Kyoto

Through the Looking Glass
A Photographic Exploration

Hae Won Shin

Buddha Rose Publications

Kyoto Through the Looking Glass
Copyright © 2018 by Hae Won Shin
All Rights Reserved.

No part of this book may be reproduced in any manner without the expressed permission of the publishing company.

First Edition 2018

ISBN 10: 1-949251-04-7
ISBN 13: 978-1-949251-04-3

Printed in the United States of America

10 9 8 7 6 5 4 3 2 1

Kyoto
Through the Looking Glass

How to use a toilet

화장실 사용법
厕所的使用方法
洗手間的使用方法
トイレのご使用方法

1

Please sit down to use this toilet.

양변기는 걸터앉아 사용하십시오.

请坐下使用马桶

請坐下使用馬桶

トイレはすわってご使用ください

2

Do not throw away the toilet paper to the trash bin. Please flush the toilet paper down the toilet instead.

휴지는 휴지통에 버리지 마시고 변기에 버려주십시오.

请不要把使用过的卫生纸扔进垃圾桶,请直接扔进马桶里冲掉

請不要把使用過的衛生紙扔進垃圾桶,請直接扔進馬桶內沖掉

トイレットペーパーはゴミいれにすてずながしてください

3

Hold your hand over the sensor to flush the toilet.

센서에 손을 대시면 자동으로 물이 내려갑니다.

冲水时用手感应一下即可

沖水時用手感應一下即可

手をかざすと水がながれます

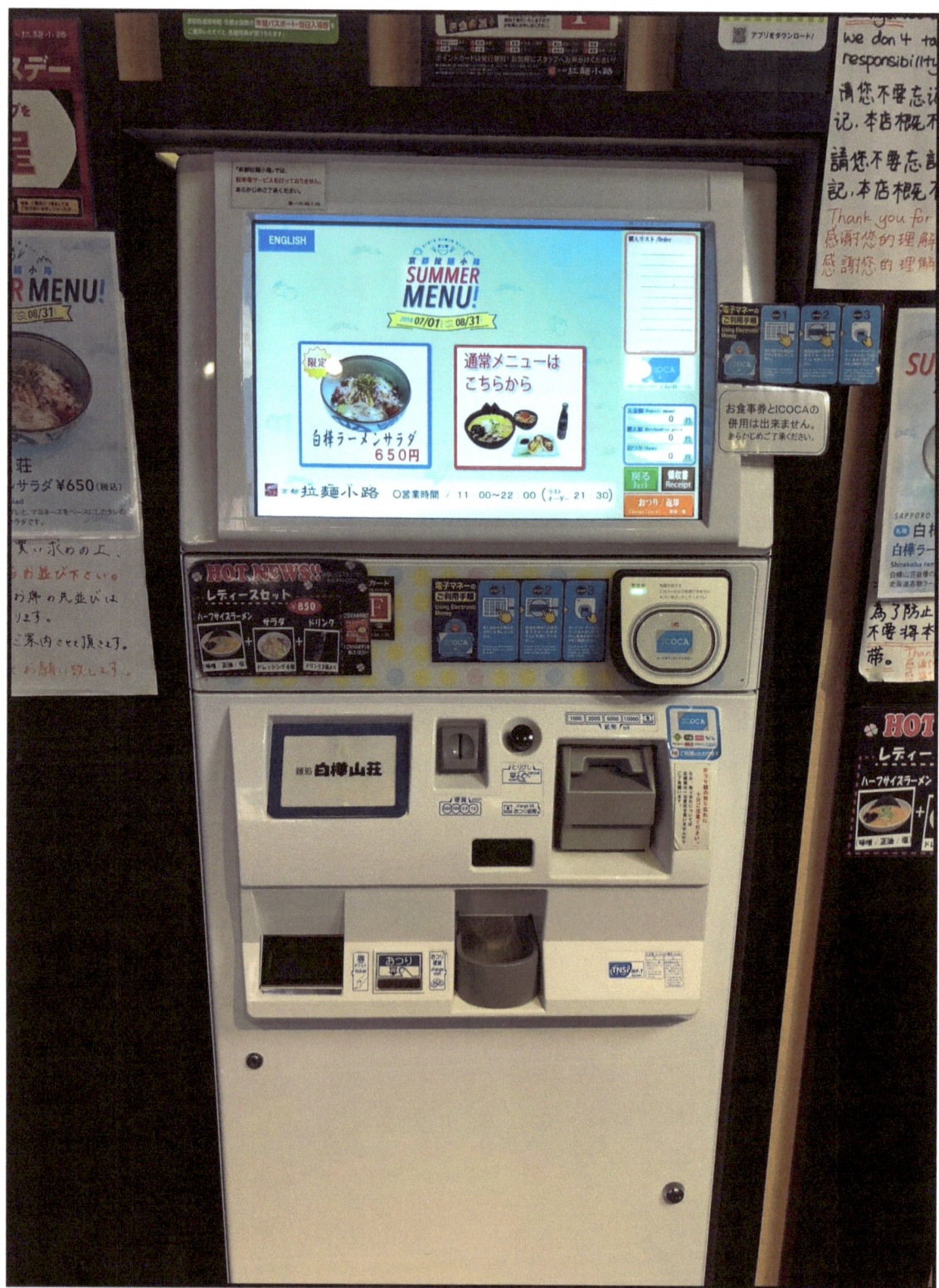

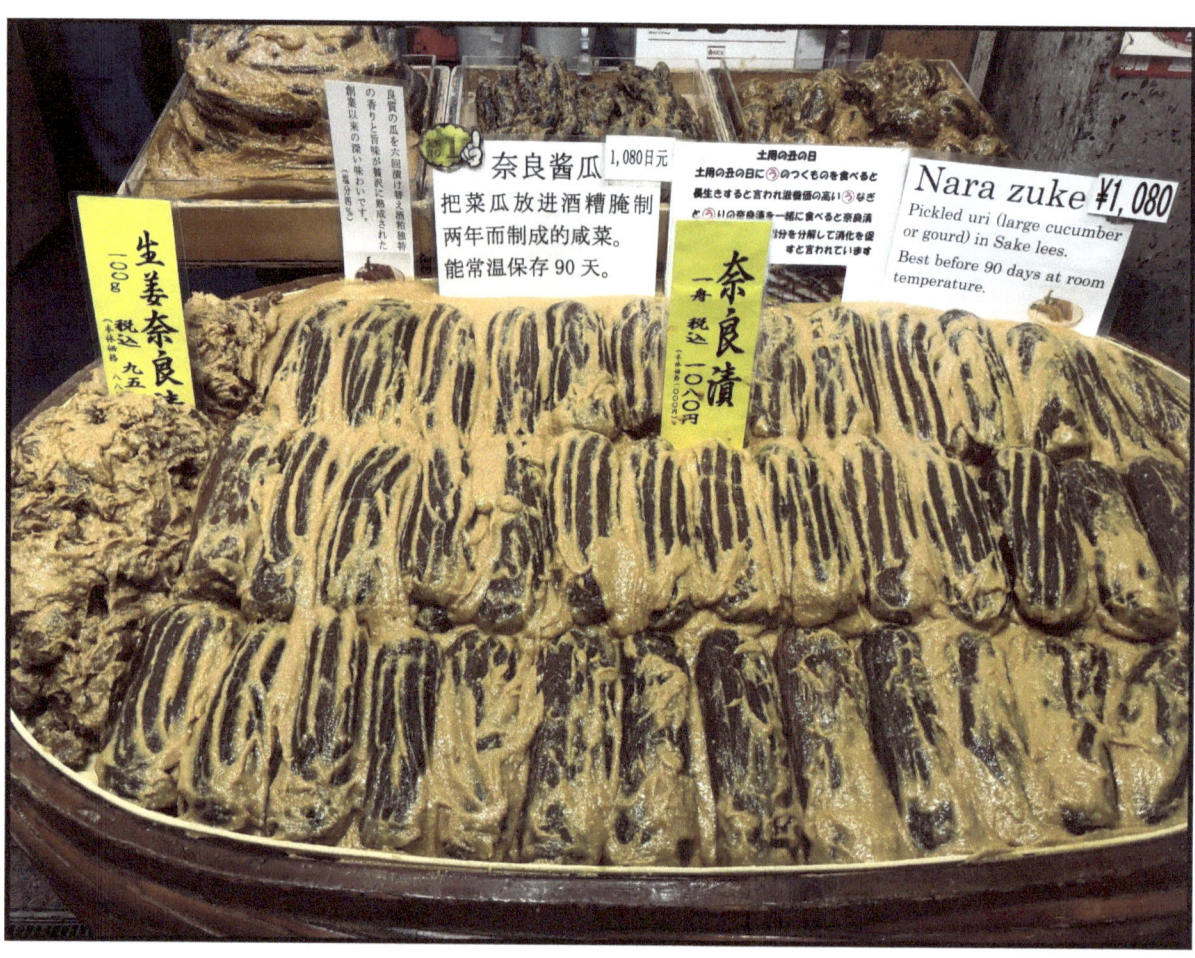

www.ingramcontent.com/pod-product-compliance
Lightning Source LLC
Chambersburg PA
CBHW041522220426
43669CB00002B/23